from: Marissa Kunz   Rachel Ray

April Min. USA   1998 (Kg.)

D0618378

from: Marissa Kunz   Rachel Ray

April Min. USA   1998 (Kg.)

DP
DEMPSEY
PARR

Lands
and People

Written by Philip Steele

Illustrated by John James

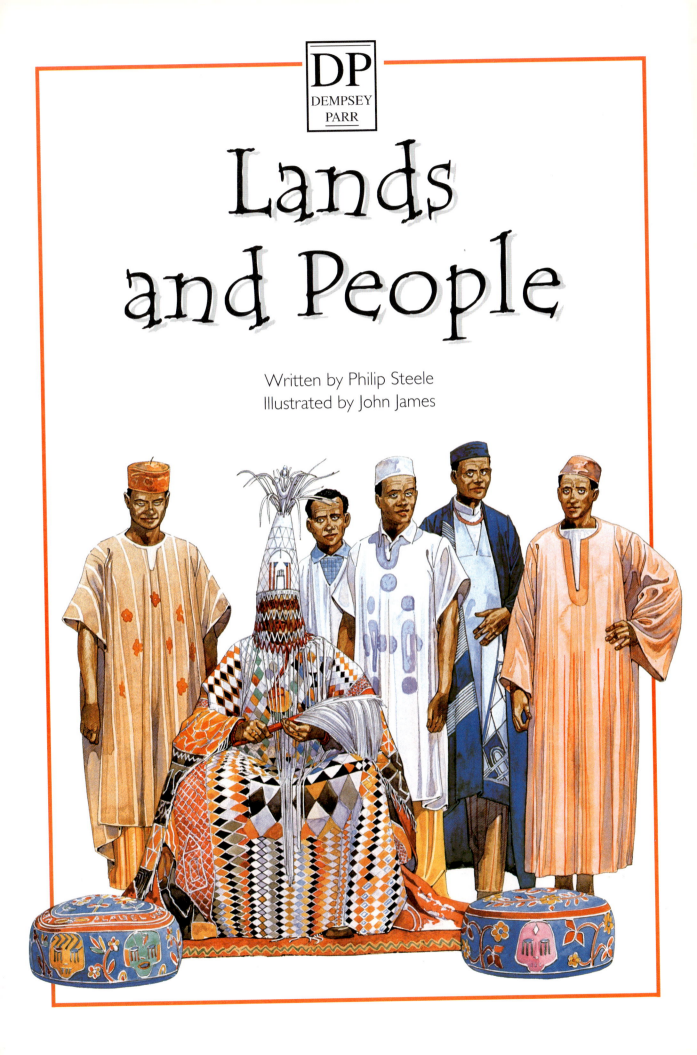

First published in Great Britain in 1998 by
Dempsey Parr
Queen Street House
4, Queen Street
Bath
BA1 1HE

Copyright © Dempsey Parr 1999

All rights reserved. No part of this publication may be reproduced,
stored in a retrieval system or transmitted, in any form or by any means,
electronic, mechanical, photocopying, recording, or otherwise,
without the prior permission of the copyright holder.

ISBN: 1-84084-409-4

Printed in Italy

Produced by Miles Kelly Publishing Ltd
Unit 11
Bardfield Centre
Great Bardfield
Essex
CM7 4SL

Designer: Diane Clouting
Editor: Linda Sonntag
Artwork commissioning: Branka Surla
Project manager: Margaret Berrill
Editorial assistant: Lynne French
with additional help from Jenni Cozens and Pat Crisp

Contents

4 The world and its people

6 Countries and flags

8 Governments and rulers

10 Keeping in touch

12 Homes and shelters

14 Living in cities

16 Getting around

18 Clothes and costumes

20 Farming and fishing

22 The food we eat

24 Trade and money

26 Faiths and religions

28 The arts

30 Festivals

32 Index

6 billion people live on Earth.

How many people live in the world?
Billions! In 1997 there were about 5,840,000,000 human beings living on our planet. That's more than twice as many as 50 years ago.

Are there more and more people?
Every minute, 167 babies are born around the world. Imagine how they would cry if they were all put together! By the year 2025 there will probably be 8,036,000,000 people in the world.

Have people always lived where they do now?
During history many peoples have moved huge distances, or migrated. The Polynesian people took 2,500 years or more to sail across the Pacific Ocean and settle its islands. People are still on the move today.

Why are some lands richer than others?
Some lands have good soil, where crops can grow. Some have oil, which is worth a lot of money. But other countries have poor soil, little rain, and no minerals. However hard people work there, they struggle to survive.

Some parts of the world are too harsh, too hot or cold for people to settle.

Frozen Arctic wastes

Where do people live?

HUMANS LIVE WHEREVER THEY CAN FIND FOOD AND WATER, which they need to stay alive. Nobody at all lives in Antarctica, the icy wilderness at the bottom of the world. Scientists do visit bases there, so that they can study rocks and icebergs and penguins. The Sahara desert in Africa is a land of burning hot sand and rocks. It has just a few places, called oases, where people can get the water they need to survive.

Have humans changed our planet ?
Over the ages, humans have changed the face of the world we live in. They have chopped down forests and dammed rivers. They have grown new plants and killed wild animals. They have built big cities and roads.

Clothes from around the world

Is there room for everybody?

Just about! But sometime in the future people may have to live in towns under the ocean or even on other planets. In those places they would need a special supply of air to stay alive.

Which country has the most people?

More people live in China than anywhere else in the world. They number about 1,237,000,000 and most of them live in the big cities of the east and the south. In the far west of China there are empty deserts and lonely mountains.

New York City

Places where many people have chosen to settle have become big cities.

How different are we from one another?

ALL HUMAN BEINGS ARE BASICALLY THE SAME, WHEREVER THEY LIVE. We may speak different languages and have different ideas. We may wear different clothes and eat different foods. Our parents may give us dark or pale skin, blue eyes or brown, or various colors of hair. But in the end we share the same needs, pleasures, hopes, and fears. We should not waste our time quarreling, for we are all members of the same big family.

What is a continent?

The big masses of land that make up the Earth's surface are called continents. The biggest continent of all is Asia, which is home to over 3.5 billion people.

Where are the most crowded places in the world?

Tiny countries and large cities may house many millions of people. The most crowded of the bigger countries is Bangladesh, with about 270 people for every square mile of land.

Who are the world's peoples?

Human beings who share the same history or language make up "a people" or "ethnic group". Sometimes many different peoples live in just one country. Over a hundred peoples live in Tanzania, each with its own way of life.

Colorful flags from around the world

Crossing the world's biggest country, 50 years ago

Which is the biggest country in the world?

The gigantic Russian Federation takes up 6,593,000 square miles of the Earth's surface. It covers two continents, Europe and Asia, and its clocks are set at 11 different times.

How long does it take to cross Russia?

It depends how you travel! These days, trains on the famous Trans-Siberian Railroad take eight days from Moscow to the Pacific coast.

Russia is so huge that when the Sun is setting over Moscow, it is rising over Vladivostock, on the Pacific coast.

The Trans-Siberian Railroad was built over a hundred years ago and opened in 1905.

What is a country?

A COUNTRY IS AN AREA OF LAND UNDER THE RULE OF A SINGLE GOVERNMENT. A country may be vast, or very small. Its borders have to be agreed with neighboring countries, although this does sometimes lead to arguments. Countries that rule themselves are called independent. Countries that are ruled by other countries are called dependencies. Sometimes several countries join up to form a single new nation, but countries may also break up into smaller nations, too.

How many dependencies are there in the world ?

Sixty-five of the world's nations are still ruled by other countries. They include many tiny islands in the Caribbean Sea and in the Atlantic and Pacific Oceans.

How many independent countries are there?

There are 192 independent countries in the world today. The number may change from one year to the next.

Swiss Guard, Vatican City

Which country fits inside a town?

The world's smallest nation is an area within the city of Rome, in Italy. It is called Vatican City and is headquarters of the Roman Catholic Church. Only a thousand or so people live there.

Where can you see all the flags of the world?

Rows and rows of colorful flags fly outside the headquarters of the United Nations in New York City. Most of the world's countries belong to this organization, which tries to solve all kinds of problems around the world.

Do all peoples have a land they can call their own?

No, the ancient homelands of some peoples are divided up between other countries. The lands of the Kurdish people are split between Turkey, Iran, and Iraq.

What are counties and states?

If you look at the map of a country, you will see that it is divided up into smaller regions. These often have their own local laws and are known as states, provinces, counties, or departments.

Refugees are people who have fled their country because of war or hunger.

Kurdish refugees

Why do countries have flags?

FLAGS CAN BE SEEN FLYING FROM BUILDINGS AND FROM BOATS. They show bold patterns and bright colors as they flutter in the wind. Many flags are badges or symbols of a nation, or of its regions. The designs on flags sometimes tell us about a country or its history. The flag of Kenya includes a traditional shield and spears, while the flag of Lebanon includes the cedar tree, which brought wealth to the region in ancient times.

India goes to the polls

More than 340 million voters took part in India's 1998 general election.

Where is the biggest general election?

Over 590 million people are allowed to vote in general elections in India. They can cast their votes at any one of over half a million polling stations set up all over the country.

Which is the world's oldest parliament?

A parliament is a meeting place where new laws are discussed and approved. The oldest parliament is in Iceland. Called the Althing, it was started by Viking settlers in AD930.

What is a head of state?

The most important person in a country is the head of state. This may be a king or a queen or an elected president.
The head of state often rides in a big car with a flag on it.

Who invented democracy?

The people of ancient Athens, in Greece, started the first democratic assembly nearly 2,500 years ago. It wasn't completely fair, as women and slaves weren't given the right to vote.

What is a republic?

It's a country that has no king or queen. France is a republic. More than 200 years ago the French king had his head chopped off, during a revolution.

Where do judges wear big wigs?

In Great Britain judges wear wigs, which were in fashion 250 years ago. This old costume is meant to show that the judge is not in court as a private person, but as someone who stands for the law of the land.

An English judge

Governments make the law, but it is up to judges to decide who has broken it.

Where might you sing along to "Jana-gana-mana" and "The Marseillaise"?

Both of them are national anthems or songs. The first tune is played to show respect to India, the second to France. You could sing along to these national anthems at important occasions, such as the Olympic Games.

Who rules the birds?

Traditionally the king or queen of England owns all the swans on the River Thames, except for those marked in a special ceremony that takes place each summer.

What is a government?

THE MEMBERS OF THE GOVERNMENT ARE THE PEOPLE WHO RUN THE COUNTRY.
They pass new laws controlling everything from schools to hospitals and businesses. Countries where the people can choose their government are called democracies. At a general election each person puts a cross on a piece of paper to make their choice known. Then their votes are counted up to see who has won. Some countries do not hold elections or have a choice of political parties. The people who rule these countries are called dictators.

Which is the world's oldest royal family?

The Japanese royal family has produced a long line of 125 reigning emperors over a period of thousands of years.

How do you recognize kings and queens?

For special ceremonies rulers wear glittering crowns and carry symbols of royal power, such as golden sticks called scepters. The beaded crown and robes shown here were worn by traditional rulers of the Yoruba people, who live in Nigeria.

Traditional robes worn by the Oba (king) of Akure, Nigeria

How does anyone get to be a king or a queen?

NORMALLY YOU HAVE TO BE A PRINCE OR PRINCESS, BORN INTO A ROYAL FAMILY with a king and queen for your mom and dad. About 800 years ago kings were very powerful people. They could have their enemies thrown into some horrible dungeon and then throw away the key. Today kings and queens have to be much nicer to people. They visit hospitals and open new bridges. They travel to meet other heads of state, as a representative of their own country.

How many languages are spoken today?

SOMEWHERE BETWEEN 5,000 AND 10,000 LANGUAGES ARE SPOKEN IN THE WORLD. Some are spoken by very few people. About 200 people in Latvia speak a language called Liv. One African language, Bikya, has only one surviving speaker. The world's most spoken language is Standard Chinese, which is used every day by 1,123,000 people. English is the world's most widespread language. It is spoken by 470 million people.

What has made the world shrink?

Of course the planet hasn't really grown smaller, it just seems that way. Today, telephones and faxes make it possible to send messages around the world instantly. Once, letters were sent by ship and took many months to arrive.

Instant communication

Telephones use satellite links to flash messages around the world.

Could we invent one language for all the world?

It's already been done! A language called Esperanto was invented over 100 years ago. Many people have learned how to speak it.

Do we all read left to right?

The Arabic language is read right-to-left, and traditional Japanese top-to-bottom.

Different cities, different signs

Many languages are related to each other and have words that sound similar.

CAHKT ПETEPOYPR
ST PETERSBURG

 አዲስ አበባ
ADDIS ABABA

What was that you whistled?

In some parts of Central America, Turkey, and the Canary Islands, people worked out a way of communicating using whistles instead of words.

Can we talk without words?

People who are unable to hear or speak can sign with their hands. Various sign languages have been developed around the world, from China to the United States.

How do we talk through space?

Satellites are machines sent into space to circle the Earth. They can pick up telephone, radio, or television signals from one part of the world and beam them down to another.

Should I stay or should I go?

Movements of the head and hands can be a kind of language. Be careful! In some countries wagging the hand palm down means "come here", but in others it means "go away". Shaking the head can mean "yes" in some countries and "no" in others.

In orbit high above the Earth, Intelsat 8 can relay 112,500 telephone conversations a day.

Each language has its own culture and traditions.

What's in a name?

In Scandinavia there's a village called Å. In New Zealand there's a place called Taumatawhakatangihangakoa-uauotamateaturipukakapikim-aungahoronukupokaiwhenuaki-tanatahu.

Methods of writing, such as alphabets, are called scripts.

Does everybody in one country speak the same language?

Not often. For example, families from all over the world have made their homes in London, the capital city of England. Their children mostly speak English at school, but at home may speak one of 275 other languages, from Turkish to Urdu.

Different scripts are used in many parts of the world.

Do we use different ways of writing?

MANY DIFFERENT KINDS OF WRITING HAVE GROWN UP around the world over the ages, using all sorts of lines and squiggles and little pictures. This book is printed in the Roman alphabet, which has 26 letters and is used for many of the world's languages. Chinese writers normally use around 5,000 different symbols, or characters, although ten times as many can be used. The Khmer alphabet, used in Cambodia, has 74 letters, while the Rotokas alphabet, used on the island of Bougainville, has only 11 letters.

What are houses made from?

MUD, STONE, SLATE, BOULDERS, BRICKS, BRANCHES, REEDS, STEEL GIRDERS sheets of iron, concrete, glass, timber planks, straw, scrap metal, turf, frozen snow, bamboo, animal hides, packing cases, cardboard boxes—you name it! All over the world people make use of whatever materials they can find or produce in order to build shelters and homes. Today many modern buildings look much the same wherever they have been built, from Brasília to Singapore. However, all sorts of local types of houses can still be seen as well.

A Dogon village, Mali

Mud huts and grain stores are built around a yard, or compound.

Where do they build mud huts?
Thatched huts with walls of dried mud can still be seen in parts of Africa, such as Mali. They are cheap to build, cool to live in and they often look beautiful too.

What are houses like in the Arctic?
Today the Inuit people of Canada mostly live in modern houses and cabins made of wood. Traditionally, their houses were made of stone and turf. They also made overnight shelters out of blocks of snow.

Which people live in caravans?
Many of Europe's Gypsies live in caravans, moving from one campsite to another. The Gypsies, who are properly known as Roma, Sinti, or Manush, arrived in Europe from India about 1,000 years ago.

Why do people live underground?
To stay cool! At Coober Pedy in Australia it is so hot that miners digging for opals built houses and even a church underground.

Bedouin nomads use camels to move from one part of the desert to another.

Houses must shelter people from cold and heat, rain and snow, storms, and floods.

Why do chalets have big roofs?

In the mountains of Switzerland, the wooden houses have broad roofs, designed for heavy falls of snow each winter.

Where do people live in caves?

The first human beings often took shelter in caves. Even today, some people in Turkey and in China still make their homes in caves. These are not cold and dripping, like Stone Age dwellings. They can be snug and very comfortable.

Reeds are used for building from South America to Southwest Asia. They are also used to thatch cottages in parts of England.

Why do people live in tents?

IN MANY PARTS OF THE WORLD PEOPLE DO NOT LIVE IN THE SAME PLACE all year round. They are nomads, following their herds of sheep and goats from one desert oasis to another, or from lowland to mountain pastures. The Bedouin are nomads who live in the dry lands of North Africa and the Near East. Their tents are woven from camel hair. Today some Bedouin have settled in towns.

Why build houses with reeds?

It makes sense to use the nearest building material to hand. Tall reeds grow in the marshes and wetlands of southern Iraq—so the Marsh Arabs who live there use them to build beautiful houses.

A tent can be packed up easily and moved from one place to another.

The Sydney Opera House has become one of the best known buildings in the world. Many tourists come from all over the world to see it.

Which famous building looks like a sailboat?

Sydney Opera House is in Australia. Its roofs rise from the blue waters of the harbor like the sails of a big yacht.

Why are landmarks useful in a city?

Each city has eye-catching buildings and monuments, which help you find your way around. Paris, in France, has the Eiffel Tower. Berlin, in Germany, has the Brandenburg Gate.

Where are the biggest cities in the world?

Which country has three capitals?

The most important city in a country is called the capital. South Africa has three of them! Cape Town is the home of the National Assembly. Pretoria is where the government offices are. Bloemfontein is the center for the law.

IN JAPAN, WHERE BIG CITIES HAVE SPREAD AND JOINED UP TO MAKE GIANT CITIES! Japan is made up of islands that have high mountains, so most people live on the flat strips of land around the coast. In order to grow, large cities have had to stretch out like ribbons until they merge into each other. More than 27 million people live in and around the capital, Tokyo. It's still growing today. On the other side of the world, Mexico City is catching up fast.

Ancient Çatal Hüyük, Turkey

Who built the first cities?

The first cities were built in Southwest Asia. Çatal Hüyük in Turkey was begun about 9,000 years ago. It had buildings of mud brick, with flat roofs, and narrow streets. About 5,000 people lived there.

Towns first grew up when people learned to farm. They no longer had to run after herds of wild animals for their food. They could stay in one place.

What problems do cities cause?

CITIES CAN BE EXCITING PLACES TO LIVE IN. THEY ARE FULL OF HUSTLE AND BUSTLE. But they often have big problems, too. So many people in one place need a lot of looking after. They need water and electricity and proper drains, fire engines and ambulances and police cars. Too much traffic often blocks up the roads and fills the air with fumes. In some countries people pour into the cities from the countryside. They cannot find work and have to live in poor conditions.

Where is the world's tallest building?
The Petronas Towers in Kuala Lumpur, Malaysia, look like two gigantic space rockets. They soar to nearly 1,483 ft (452 meters), making up the tallest building in the world.

Which is the world's oldest capital?
Damascus, capital of Syria, has been lived in for about 4,500 years.

How does this ancient town differ from a modern one?

Cities became centres of trade, where people made pottery, baskets, food, tools and clothes.

Where is the Big Apple?
This is a popular nickname for New York City. So go ahead and take a bite!

Who lives at the ends of the Earth?
One of the world's most northerly settlements is Ny-Alesund, in the Arctic territory of Svalbard. The southernmost is Puerto Williams in Tierra del Fuego, Chile.

Which is the highest city?
Lhasa stands 12,086 ft (3,684 meters) above sea level. It is the capital city of Tibet, a region in the Himalaya Mountains that is governed by China. Tibet is sometimes called the "roof of the world".

Why was London Bridge falling down?
Children today still sing a rhyme that says "London Bridge is falling down." It's a very old song. The ancient bridge over the River Thames was pulled down by a Viking called Olaf the Stout—nearly a thousand years ago!

Which city is named after a goddess?
Athens, the capital of Greece, shares its name with an ancient goddess called Athene. Her beautiful temple, the Parthenon, still towers over the modern city. It was built in 438BC.

How do you cross the Arctic snow?

You could always ride on a sled pulled by a team of dogs, as in the old days. But most people today ride snowmobiles, which are a bit like motorcycles with runners instead of wheels.

In Siberia, snowmobiles can use solid frozen rivers as roads during the winter months.

Crossing the Russian Arctic

Where can you catch a train into the sky?

In the Andes mountains of South America. One track in Peru climbs to 15,807 ft (4,818 meters) above sea level. In Salta, Argentina. you can catch another high-rise locomotive, known as the "Train to the Clouds."

Where was a hot-air balloon first flown?

The place was Paris, the capital of France, and the year was 1783. The passengers were, believe it or not, a sheep, a dog, and a duck! Later, people tried out the balloon for themselves.

Chinese junk

What is the world's longest road?

THE PAN-AMERICAN HIGHWAY. IT STARTS AT THE TOP OF THE WORLD, IN THE CHILLY HEART OF Alaska. It then heads on through Canada and the United States to the steamy forests of Central America. There is still a bit missing in the middle, but the road starts up again and continues all the way down through South America to Chile, looping around to Argentina and Brazil. The total distance? Almost 15,000 miles (24,000 km).

Where is the world's biggest airport?
Riyadh airport in Saudi Arabia is bigger than some countries. It covers 87 square miles (225 sq km) of the Arabian desert.

Where are boats used as buses?
In the beautiful Italian city of Venice, there are canals instead of roads. People travel from one part of the city to another by boat.

What is a caravan and where might you travel in one?
A caravan is a group of traders who cross the desert by camel. Camels are able to carry people across the Sahara for six days without needing a drink of water.

Where are the longest trucks?
In the outback, the dusty back country of Australia, the roads are long and straight and pretty empty. Trucks can hitch on three or four giant trailers to form a "road train."

Australian road train

A road train speeds across the Nullarbor Desert in southern Australia.

Traditional wooden boats still sail along the Hong Kong waterfront.

How can you travel underneath the Alps?

THE ALPS ARE SNOWY MOUNTAINS THAT RUN ACROSS FRANCE, ITALY, Switzerland and Austria. They soar to 16,000 ft (4,810 meters) above sea level at Mont Blanc. In the days of ancient Rome a general named Hannibal tried to cross the Alps with 34 war elephants! Today, tunnels carry trains and cars through the heart of the mountains. The St. Gotthard tunnel in Switzerland is the world's longest road tunnel, over 10 miles (16 km) long.

Many countries still use wooden boats. Dhows sail off Arabia and East Africa, and feluccas are used on the River Nile.

What is a junk?
It is a big wooden ship, traditionally built in China. Its big sails are strengthened by strips of wood. Junks aren't as common as they used to be, but they can still be seen on the South China Sea.

17

African mask

This mask is worn at special ceremonies in Baluba, Africa.

Where is the capital of fashion?
Milan, London, New York, and many other cities stage fantastic fashion shows each year. But Paris, in France, has been the center of world fashion for hundreds of years.

What is batik?
This is a way of making pretty patterns on cloth. Wax is put on the fiber so that the dye sinks in only in certain places. This method was invented in Java, Indonesia.

Do people still wear national costume?
Most people in the world today wear T-shirts and jeans, skirts, or suits. Only on special occasions do they still put on traditional costumes of their region. In some countries, however, people still wear their local style of dress every day.

Clothes today may be made from natural fibers such as wool, silk, or cotton, or from artificial fibers such as nylon and plastic.

How do people dress in hot countries?

IN HOT COUNTRIES PEOPLE PROTECT THEIR HEADS FROM THE SUN WITH all kinds of broad-brimmed hats, from the Mexican sombrero to the cone-shaped straw hats worn by farm workers in southern China and Vietnam. They may wear robes like the Arabs, or loose fitting cotton trousers. In desert lands people may cover their heads with cloths, to keep out the sand. The Tuareg of the Sahara wrap scarves around the face until only the eyes can be seen. Their name means "the veiled people."

Which ladies wear tall lace hats?
The Breton people of northwest Europe are proud of their costume, which they wear for special occasions. The men wear vests and big black hats. The women wear lace caps, some of which are high and shaped like chimneys.

Where do Panama hats come from?

Actually, Panama hats were first made in Ecuador, where they were plaited from the leaves of the jipijapa palm. They were first exported, or shipped abroad, from Panama, which is why they are now called Panama hats.

Today it is not always easy to tell where people come from by the clothes they wear.

How do we keep warm and dry?

SINCE PREHISTORIC TIMES, PEOPLE HAVE USED FUR AND ANIMAL SKINS TO KEEP out the cold. In the Arctic today, the Inuit people still often wear traditional clothes made from fur, sealskin or caribou (reindeer) hide. The Saami people of northern Finland also use their reindeer herds to provide leather goods. Wool, woven into textiles or pressed into felt, is used wherever the weather is cold. It is a good warm fibre, and the natural oils in it keep out the rain—that's why sheep don't shrink!

Who invented silk?

The Chinese were the first people to make silk, from the cocoons of silkworms, thousands of years ago. Today silk may be used to make beautiful Indian wraps called saris and Japanese robes called kimonos.

Where do soldiers wear skirts?

Guards of honor in the Greek army are called Evzónes. Their uniform is based on the old-fashioned costume of the mountain peoples—a white kilt, woolen leggings and a cap with a tassel.

Who are the true cloggies?

A hundred years ago wooden shoes, or clogs, were worn in many parts of Europe. The most famous clogs were the Dutch ones, which are still often worn today by farmers and market traders in the Netherlands.

Who wears feathers to a singsing?

A singsing is a big festival, Papua New Guinea style. Men paint their faces and wear ornaments of bone and shell and bird-of-paradise feathers. Traditional dress may include skirts made of leaves and grass.

Who are the Gauchos?

The cowboys of the Pampas, which are the grasslands of Argentina. Once the Gauchos were famous for their wild way of life. Today they still round up the cattle on big ranches called estancias.

Where are the world's biggest ranches?

The world's biggest sheep and cattle stations are in the Australian outback. The best way to cross these lands is in a light aircraft.

How can barren deserts be turned green?

Water can be piped into desert areas so that crops will grow there. But this irrigation can be very expensive and the water can also wash salts from the soil, making it difficult to grow plants.

Where do farmers grow coconuts?

Coconut fruits are big and green— the bit we buy in shops is just the brown seed inside. The white flesh inside the nut may be dried and sold as copra. Coconut palms grow best on the shores of the Indian and Pacific Oceans.

Which were the first all-American crops?

Six hundred years ago, nobody in Europe had ever seen potatoes, corn or tomatoes. These important food crops were first developed by the peoples who lived in the Americas before European settlers arrived there.

What grows best in floods and soggy wet mud?

RICE KEEPS THE WORLD ALIVE. BILLIONS OF PEOPLE EAT IT EVERY DAY, ESPECIALLY in Asia. Grains of rice are the seeds of a kind of grass that grows wild in wet river valleys. To cultivate it, farmers plant out the seedlings in flooded fields called paddies. In hilly lands, terraces are cut in the hillsides and the water flows down channels in the muddy soil.

Terraced rice fields

Some rice terraces, like these in the Philippines, are thousands of years old.

The fish swim into the nets when they are lowered into the water. The nets are then swung into the air and emptied.

Scoop nets

What is a cash crop?
It is any crop that is sold for money. Many small farmers around the world can only grow enough food to feed themselves and their families, without having any to spare.

Where do fishermen use hoops and scoops?
Giant fishing nets like these can be lowered from the shore into lakes and seas. They are often used in China and India.

Are there enough fish in the sea?
Modern boats catch so many fish that in many places fish have become scarce. Some of the richest fishing grounds were off Newfoundland, in the North Atlantic Ocean. Fishing there has now been banned until the numbers recover.

Combine harvester

What is the sweetest crop of all?
Sugarcane is grown on many islands in the Caribbean region. In Barbados, the end of the cane harvest is marked by Cropover, a grand celebration with music, dancing and parades.

Basic foods such as wheat (above) and rice are called staple crops.

Modern types of rice can produce several harvests a year. They can be planted by machines, but these are too expensive for many farmers.

Where are the world's breadbaskets?

IMPORTANT WHEAT-PRODUCING AREAS OF THE WORLD ARE CALLED "BREADBASKETS" because they provide us with the bread we eat each day. Wheat is a kind of grass, and so it grows best in areas which were once natural grasslands. These include the prairies of Canada and the United States and the steppes of Ukraine and southern Russia. Huge combine harvesters move across the prairies for days and weeks on end, cutting the wheat and separating out the grain.

How do we keep food fresh?

TODAY, BUTTER CAN BE SENT TO EUROPE ALL THE WAY FROM NEW ZEALAND— kept cool by refrigeration. The first ever refrigerator ship was invented in 1877 to carry beef from Argentina. But how did people keep food fresh before that? The old methods were simpler—pickling, smoking, or drying. The Native Americans dried meat in the sun and mixed it with fruit to make pemmican for their travels. Traditional methods are still used today to produce some of the world's tastiest foods—Indian pickles and chutneys, Irish smoked salmon, or Italian sun-dried tomatoes.

How much seaweed can you eat?
Various seaweeds are eaten in Japan, and in South Wales seaweed makes up a dish called laverbread. A seaweed called carrageen moss is often used to thicken ice cream and milk puddings. Seaweed is also found in toothpaste!

How do you eat with chopsticks?
Chopsticks are popular in China and Japan. Hold one stick between the thumb and the bottom of the first two fingers. Hold the other stick farther along the first two fingers and support it with the third. It's easy!

The food people eat depends not just on the crops they can grow, the animals they can raise, or the fish they can catch, but also on their traditional customs and religious beliefs.

Who invented noodles?
Which noodles came first—Italian spaghetti or Chinese chow mein? Some people say that the traveler Marco Polo brought the secret of noodle-making back to Italy from China in the Middle Ages. No! say others—the Romans were making pasta in Italy long before that. Maybe it was invented in both places.

Fresh foods from around the world

What is caviar?
One of the most expensive foods in the world. It is made of eggs from a fish called the sturgeon, which lives in lakes and rivers in Russia and other northern lands.

What is yerba maté?
It is a bitter but refreshing hot drink, made from the leaves of the Paraguay holly. It is sipped from a gourd (a kind of pumpkin shell) through a silver straw, and is very popular in Argentina.

Many southern Indian dishes are vegetarian. Some people in other parts of the world also prefer not to eat meat.

What is jambalaya?
Rice for a start, then shrimp and peppers, all in an amazing hot spicy sauce. Where is this served up? New Orleans, in the steamy south of Louisiana.

Who wrote a poem to his haggis?
Robert Burns, Scotland's greatest poet, who lived in the 1700s. The haggis is a traditional dish from Scotland. It is made up of lamb's heart, liver, and lungs, suet, onions and oatmeal cooked inside—guess what—a sheep's stomach!

Where do you buy milk by the kilo?
In the Russian Arctic it is so cold in winter that milk is sold in frozen chunks rather than by the liter.

What is the most delicious food?

HAUTE CUISINE IS FRENCH, AND IT MEANS HIGH-QUALITY COOKING. People all over the world love French food. But is it really the most delicious food in the world? Chinese cooking is also thought to be a fine art. But really, which food we like or dislike is just a question of personal taste. Sheeps' eyeballs, insect grubs, snakes, and pigs' ears can all be found on menus in one part of the world or another—and many people find them absolutely mouthwatering.

Preparing an African meal
African dishes are often based on cornmeal, and served with spicy vegetables, fish, or meat.

Who makes the world's hottest curries?
The people of southern India. A mouthwatering recipe might include fiery spices such as red chilli pepper and fresh hot green chillies, ginger, garlic, turmeric, and curry leaves.

Where were banknotes invented?
Paper money was first used in China, a thousand years ago.

More and more people around the world use plastic cards to pay for goods.

What are currencies?
A currency is a money system, such as the Japanese yen, the US dollar, the Mongolian tugrik, or the Bhutan ngultrum. The exchange rate is what it costs to buy or sell one currency for another.

Plastic, a new form of money

Where is the Silk Road?
This is an ancient trading route stretching all the way from China through Central Asia to the Mediterranean Sea. Hundreds of years ago, silk, tea and spices were transported along this road to the West by camel and pony trains.

Who catches smugglers?
If you wish to take some goods from one country to another, you might have to pay a tax to the government. Customs officers may check your luggage to see that you are not sneaking in—or smuggling—illegal goods.

Who makes the most money?
The mint—that's the place where coins and banknotes are made. The United States treasury in Philadelphia produces billions of new coins each year.

Why sell stamps on Pitcairn?
Only 50 or so people live on remote Pitcairn Island, in the Pacific Ocean. So why do the islanders print so many postage stamps? Well, they sell them to stamp collectors and this make them a lot of money.

Where do people do business?

IN NIGERIA, MONEY CHANGES HANDS EVERY DAY IN THE BUSY TOWN MARKET.
Laid out on the ground are batteries, watches, embroidered hats, peanuts, yams, and cans of fish. The customers haggle with the women selling the goods, arguing about the price. In England trading might take in a big supermarket, packed with Saturday morning shoppers. In Switzerland bankers watch their computer screens to check their profits. In the New York stock exchange, traders grab their telephones as they buy and sell shares in companies. It's all in a day's work.

Where do you buy your food? At a city store or in a traditional street market?

What can people use as money?

TODAY EVERY COUNTRY IN THE WORLD USES COINS AND PAPER BANK NOTES, although goods may still be swapped rather than bought in many regions. Over the ages all kinds of other things have been used as money around the world—shells, large stones, beads, salt, tobacco, blocks of tea, sharks' teeth, or cocoa beans. These had no value in themselves, but then neither do the metal, paper or plastic we use today. They are just tokens of exchange.

Where in the world are there floating markets?
In Thailand and other parts of Southeast Asia, traders often sell vegetables, fruit, flowers, and spices from small boats called sampans, which are moored along river banks and jetties.

Street market, India

An Indian trader waits for customers to buy her fresh produce. Among her wares are okra, tomatoes, beans, cauliflower, mooli, peppers, and lemons.

What are the five "K's"?

Sikh men honor five religious traditions. Kesh is uncut hair, worn in a turban. They carry a Kangha, or comb, a Kkara or metal bangle, and a Kirpan or dagger. They wear an undergarment called a Kaccha.

Which city is holy to three faiths?

Jerusalem is a holy place for Jews, Muslims and Christians. Sacred sites include the Western Wall, the Dome of the Rock and the Church of the Holy Sepulcher.

Stained glass window

This round window—called a rose window—in Lincoln Cathedral, England, is made of beautiful stained glass.

Where do young boys become monks?

In Myanmar a four year-old boy learns about the life of Buddha at a special ceremony. He is dressed as a rich prince and is then made to wear the simple robes of a Buddhist monk.

Where do pilgrims go?

PILGRIMS ARE RELIGIOUS PEOPLE WHO TRAVEL TO HOLY PLACES AND SHRINES around the world. Muslims try to travel to the sacred city of Mecca, in Saudi Arabia, at least once in their lifetime. Hindus may travel to the city of Varanasi, in India, to wash in the holy waters of the River Ganges. Christians travel to Bethlehem, the birthplace of Jesus Christ, or to the great cathedrals built in Europe during the Middle Ages, such as Santiago de Compostela in Spain.

What is Diwali?

This is the time in the autumn when Hindus celebrate their new year and honor Lakshmi, goddess of good fortune. Candles are lit in windows and people give each other cards and presents.

The lamps of Diwali

Lighted candles mark the feast of Diwali. The Hindu religion grew up in India many thousands of years ago.

Why do people fast?

IN MANY RELIGIONS PEOPLE FAST, OR GO WITHOUT FOOD, AS PART OF THEIR WORSHIP. If you visit a Muslim city sich as Cairo or Algiers during Ramadan, the ninth month of the Islamic year, you will find that no food is served during daylight hours. Many Christians also give up eating certain foods during Lent, the days leading up to Holy Week, when they think about the death of Jesus. In Spain, during Holy Week, Christians carry crosses and religious statues in street processions.

What is Shinto?
This is the ancient religion of Japan. At its holy shrines people pray for happiness and to honour their ancestors. Many Japanese people also follow Buddhist beliefs.

What is Hanukkah?
This Jewish festival of light lasts eight days. Families light a new candle each day on a special candlestick called a menorah. Hanukkah celebrates the recapture of the temple in Jerusalem in ancient times.

Why is Mount Athos important?
This rocky headland in northern Greece is holy to Christians of the Eastern Orthodox faith. Monks have worshipped here since the Middle Ages. They wear beards, tall black hats, and robes.

Muslim prayers
Muslims pray to God (Allah) five times a day. The most important worship is at noon on Friday.

Which country has the most Muslims?
Indonesia is the largest Islamic country in the world, although some parts of it, such as the island of Bali, are mostly Hindu.

Light and fire are important symbols of the holy spirit in many religions.

What is the Tao?
It is said "dow" and it means "the way". It is the name given to the beliefs of the Chinese thinker Lao Zi, who lived about 2,600 years ago. Taoists believe in the harmony of the universe.

Which priests cover their mouths?
Some priests of the Jain religion, in India, wear masks over their mouths. This is because they respect all living things and do not wish to harm or swallow even the tiniest insect that might fly into their mouths.

Who was Confucius?
This is the English name given to the Chinese thinker Kong Fuzi, who lived at the same time as Lao Zi. His beliefs in an ordered society and respect for ancestors became very popular in China.

What are Parsis?
The Parsi religion began long ago in ancient Persia, now Iran. Many of its followers fled to India more than 1,000 years ago and are now found in many countries around the world.

Aboriginal art, Australia

Like dance and theater, art often has its origins in religious and magical rituals.

Who paints pictures of the dreamtime?

Australia's Aborigines look back to the dreamtime, a magical age when the world was being formed, along with its animals and peoples. They paint wonderful pictures of it.

Where do they dance like the gods?

Kathakali is a kind of dance drama performed in Kerala, southern India. Dancers in masks and gorgeous costumes act out ancient tales of gods and demons.

Why do people love to dance?

DANCING IS A VERY DRAMATIC WAY OF EXPRESSING FEELINGS OF EVERY KIND. In Spain, passionate flamenco dancers stamp and click their fingers to guitar music. In England, morris dancers happily jingle bells tied to their legs and wave sticks. In Africa there are important dances for growing up and for funerals. The first dances of all were probably designed to bring good fortune to prehistoric hunters, where a priest put on the skins and horns of the animal his people wanted to kill.

Who sings in Beijing?

Beijing opera is quite a performance! Musicians bang cymbals together and actors sing in high voices. They take the part of heroes and villains in ancient Chinese tales. Their faces are painted and they wear beautiful costumes with long pheasant feathers.

Where is the world's biggest art gallery?

At St. Petersburg in Russia. It is made up of two great buildings, the Hermitage and the Winter Palace, and these hold millions of exhibits.

Mbuti dancers

Young Mbuti people from Zaire decorate their bodies with white makeup for a dance to celebrate the beginning of adulthood.

Where do drums talk?

The tama is nicknamed the "talking drum". Its tightness can be varied while it is being played, to make a strange throbbing sound. It is played in Senegal and the Gambia, in Africa.

Where is the world's very oldest theater?

THE OLDEST THEATER STILL IN USE TODAY IS CALLED THE TEATRO OLIMPICO and it is at Vicenza, in Italy. It opened over 400 years ago. But people were going to see plays long, long before that. In ancient Greece people went to see masked actors appear in some of the funniest and saddest plays ever written, at open-air theaters made of stone. These can still be seen today all over Greece.

What is kabuki?
Kabuki is an exciting type of drama that became popular in Japan in the 1600s and may still be seen today. The actors wear splendid makeup and costumes.

Kabuki—Japanese theatre

In kabuki, all the parts are played by male actors, some dressed up as beautiful women.

Who dances a hakka?
In New Zealand young Maori people have kept alive many of their traditional dances. The hakka was a dance for warriors, to bring them strength to face the battles ahead.

Where is Stratford?
Well, there are two Stratfords. Four hundred years ago, Stratford-upon-Avon, in England, was the home of one of the most famous playwrights who ever lived, William Shakespeare. The other Stratford in Ontario, Canada, holds a drama festival every year in his honor.

Who plays the "pans"?
People in the Caribbean, at carnival time. The "pans" are the steel drums, which can produce beautiful dance rhythms and melodies.

Who makes pictures from sand?
The Navaho people of the southwestern United States make beautiful patterns using many different colored sands.

Fireworks were invented long ago in China.

What is a powwow?
It means "get-together" in Algonkian. The Native American peoples of the United States and the First Nations of Canada meet up at powwows each year to celebrate their traditions with dance and music.

Where is the bun festival?
On the Chinese island of Cheung Chau, near Hong Kong, there is a big festival each May, with parades and religious ceremonies. During the celebrations people climb up huge towers made of buns.

What is carnival?

IN ANCIENT ROME THERE WAS A ROWDY WINTER FESTIVAL CALLED SATURNALIA. People copied this idea in the Middle Ages. They feasted and had fun before the dark, cold days of Lent began, when Christians had to give up eating meat. People still celebrate carnival today. In Germany there are wild parties and in Venice, Italy, people wear elegant masks and cloaks. In New Orleans, in Louisiana, jazz bands parade in the streets. In Trinidad and in Rio de Janeiro, Brazil, people dance wearing sparkling fancy dress and let off spectacular fireworks.

Who rides to the Feria?
Each April the people of Seville, in Spain, ride on horseback to a grand fair on the banks of the River Guadalquivir. They wear traditional finery and dance all night.

Who gets to sit in the leader's chair?
In Turkey, April 23 is Children's Day. A child even gets the chance to sit at the desk of the country's prime minister! There are puppet shows, dances, and a kite-flying competition.

Dragon dance

At the Chinese New Year people parade through the streets wearing the skin of a mighty dragon.

Where do dragons dance?

WHEREVER CHINESE PEOPLE GET TOGETHER TO CELEBRATE their New Year or Spring Festival. The lucky dragon weaves in and out of the streets, held up by the people crouching underneath its long body. Firecrackers go bang, to scare away evil spirits. The festival is a chance for families to get together, give each other presents and wish each other good fortune for the year ahead.

The festival of Holi

Hindu children throw colored powder over each other at the spring festival.

Who wears green on St. Patrick's Day?
St. Patrick's Day, on March 17, is the national day of Ireland. It is celebrated wherever Irish people have settled over the ages, from the United States to Australia. People wear green clothes or put green shamrock leaves in their buttonholes.

Who remembers the fifth of November?
People in Great Britain. The date recalls the capture of Guy Fawkes, who plotted to blow up the Houses of Parliament in London nearly 400 years ago. The night is marked by blazing bonfires, fireworks, and home-made toffee.

Where is New Year's Day always wet?
In Myanmar people celebrate the Buddhist New Year by splashing and spraying water over their friends!

Index

A

Aborigines 28
Africa 4, 10, 12, 18, 23, 28
Alaska 16
Algiers 27
alphabet 11
Alps 17
Andes Mountains 16
Antarctica 4
Arabia 17
Arabs 10, 13, 18
Arctic 4, 15, 16, 19, 23
Argentina 16, 20, 22
art 28, 29
Asia 5, 6, 13, 14, 20, 24, 25
Athens 8, 15
Atlantic Ocean 6, 21
Australia 12, 17, 20, 28
Austria 17

B

Bangladesh 5
Barbados 21
Bedouin 13
Bethlehem 26
birth rate 4
Brazil 12, 16, 30
buildings 12, 14, 15
Burns, Robert 23

C

Cairo, Egypt 27
Cambodia 11
Canada 12, 16, 21, 30
Canary Islands 10
caravan 12, 17
Caribbean Sea, 21
Çatal Hüyük, Turkey 14
Central America 10, 16
Chile 15, 16
China 5, 13, 15, 18, 21, 28
    festivals 30, 31
    food 22, 23
    junks 16, 17
    language 10, 11
    money 24
    religion 27
    silk 19, 24
cities 5, 12, 14, 15, 17
communication 10, 11
Confucius 27
costume 4, 5, 18, 19, 28
countries 6, 7
currency 24

D

dances 28
democracies 8

EFG

East Africa 17
Ecuador 19
election 8
England 8, 11, 13, 24, 28
Esperanto language 10
ethnic groups 5
Europe 6, 12, 18, 19, 22

farming 20, 21
Fawkes, Guy 31
festivals 27, 30, 31
Finland 19
flags 6, 7
food 22, 23
France 8, 16, 17, 18, 23

Germany 30
government 6, 8, 14, 24
Great Britain 8, 31
Greece 8, 15, 19, 27
Gypsies 12

HI

Hannibal 17
Himalaya Mountains 15
Hong Kong 17, 30
houses 12, 13
human beings 4, 5, 13

Iceland 8
India 8, 12, 19, 21, 25
    dance 28
    food 22, 23
    religion 26, 27
Indian Ocean 20
Indonesia 18, 27
Inuit 12, 19
Iran 27
Iraq 7, 13
Ireland 22, 31
Italy 7, 17, 22, 30

JKLM

Japan 9, 10, 14, 19, 22, 27
Jerusalem 25, 27
junk 16, 17

Kenya 7
Kurdish people 7

language 5, 10, 11
laws 8, 14
Lebanon 7
London, England 11, 15, 18, 31

Malaysia 15
Mediterranean Sea 24
Mexico 14, 18
migration 4
money 24, 25
Mongolia 24
Myanmar 26, 31

NO

nations 6, 7, 8
Native American peoples 22, 30

Netherlands 19
New Orleans 23, 30
New York City 5, 7, 15, 18, 24
New Zealand 11, 22
Newfoundland 21
Nigeria 9, 24
nomads 13
North Africa 13
North Atlantic Ocean 21

PQR

Pacific Ocean 4, 6, 20, 24
Pan-American Highway 16
Papua New Guinea 19
peoples 5, 7
Peru 16
Philippines 20
Polo, Marco 22
Polynesia 4
population 4, 5

refugees 7
religion 26, 27, 28, 30, 31
roads 16, 17
Roman Catholic Church 7
Rome 7, 11, 22, 30
rulers 6, 8, 9
Russian Federation 6, 16, 21, 22, 23, 28

S

Sahara desert, Africa 4, 17, 18
satellites 10, 11
Saudi Arabia 17, 26
Scandinavia 11
Scotland 23
Siberia 16
Singapore 12
South Africa 14
South America 13, 16
South Wales 22
Spain 26, 27, 28, 30
Switzerland 13, 17, 24
Syria 15

T

Tanzania 5
Thailand 25
Tibet 15
trade 15, 24, 25
trains 6, 16, 17
Trinidad 30
Tuareg 18
Turkestan 7
Turkey 10, 11, 13, 14, 30

UVWXYZ

Ukraine 21
United Nations 7
United States of America 8, 12, 16, 21, 24, 30

Vatican City 7
Vietnam 18